CINNAMON THEOLOGIES

CINNAMON THEOLOGIES

∾

99 Sonnets by
STEVEN NIGHTINGALE

RAINSHADOW EDITIONS
THE BLACK ROCK PRESS
2008

Cloth Edition:

978-1-891033-40-7

Trade Paper Edition:

978-1-891033-42-1

Library of Congress Control Number:

2008924321

The Black Rock Press

University of Nevada, Reno Reno, NV 89557-0044

www.blackrockpress.org

Printed in the United States of America

First Edition

For Lucia and Gabriella

—mi canción, mi esperanza, mi tierra

Contents

Introduction

WHAT IS A SONNET? What might it be to you, to me; what might it mean?

It is a tall window we throw open, to look upon another and a better world.

It is an enchanted house. You enter, step by step and word by word, and come upon strangers who help you, cherish you. You talk with them in a room whose wood grain holds the rhythm of a song you remember at last; the fire in the hearth lights the past and the future.

It is a ship we learn to sail, pulling the lines into our understanding the way sailors pull line to trim sails; so to move in concord with the clear heavens.

It is a record of the moment you walk around a corner and see plain fact, the world beyond any idea of ourselves, a forthright world waiting for us everywhere. You round that corner and see a meteor shower moving in the street, a wild river flashing in the sunlight; the child you adore, a flower whose petals enfold a fine old story, a mountain range whose canyons show a light made sweet by rough country.

And all this, just the beginning of our adventures...

As with the previous two books of sonnets, these poems were written in a miscellany of places; many of them in Spain, in our beloved Albayzin, a barrio in the city of Granada, where even the cobblestones hold stanzas; in Tarifa, further south, on the windblown beach, with the mountains of Morocco calling from across the Strait of Gibraltar; in the city of Fez, which is a honeycomb of beauties; in India, near a marketplace that sold big rocks of sugar, not far from a stand where families buy wood to burn their dead; in Lemon Canyon of the Sierra Nevada, sitting close by our sleeping newborn daughter; and in my beloved home state of Nevada, at campsites far out in the high desert, where the Milky Way can still crease your forehead. All through such travels, I had with me a battered notebook of sonnets, which I held to as a man in peril holds on to a lifeline thrown him.

In the many readings I have given of such verse, I have enjoyed a persistent question, to wit: Why take so much time with such an old form? Because sonnets are a lifeline, thrown to all of us by the centuries. If we are not to perish in the violence and idiocy of history, then we do well to hold fast to a form that can concentrate grace, understanding, and laughter.

I think of you, reader, sitting in the light of the morning with a book of poems, reading aloud to someone you love. All the outlandish beauties of the world travel toward you, toward the two of you.

The darkness of history will yield; but only to your powers and sweetness.

S. N.
Granada, July 2007

Let's Say

Say, a child bearing rainbows, a canyon
Made into music by a river, old reason

Alone in a cafe, watching the sunlight.
Say, in anonymous clouds of midwinter,
Lovely mysterious sisters, who at night

With elfin cosmic tools knit snowflakes
By the easy billion, then go to pray
For more fun. Say, you form windbreaks
Out of words. Say, a musky lover gave

You storms from a rain-forest, a pair
Of macaws, orquestral butterflies, a cure.
Say that sorrow learned of light and air

That you had come-hither hope, a song,
News of what you are, where you belong—

Not To Say That the Light Is Alive

A tissue of light, in love, moves on
To make cactus, pimento, the dawn,

Toucan, ocean, the hand of a little girl
Who sees how galaxies turn with her.
It is to light that the worlds refer.

You and I, are what light endures.
Everything is traveling. Within a stone,
A word, languor of a cat, the whispers
Of an aria, philosophy, ice cream cone,

We find one story, woven together
With brilliant movement, dance, curl,
And the cyclone's whirl, rough measure

Of heaven, wheeling galaxy, mote of dust—
Worlds move, to see who light can trust.

All of Us, a Leaf, Springtime

What if one leaf on a river willow
In spring, were a sign you follow

Because memory, which has in it
A future, sees the modest, green arc
Of a vault in paradise; sees the wit

Of a working season—supple amorous genius,
Coloratura and symposium of propositions,
Savory prayer, strategy and joke of dust,
Volcanic wink of beauty, spiced reasons,

Old suavities? What if, after being a fool,
You may know redemption, bear the mark
Made by a willow leaf one day, in the cool

Of a morning, upon soul, sense, face?
Spiritual tattoo, like the earth in space.

What the Seamstress Is Thinking

Is there a sweetness that comes not
From understanding? What we sought

Comes wildly from conscious light,
The fine old inside joke of the sun.
What was ignorant, barbarous sight—

Now, conception: mind, world marry.
What you see is what you may be.
Flesh, soul move together amorously.
Even in the dirt, lustrous unity.

We are told we must suffer, yet
What misery remains, every gun
Is full of nutmeg, your history inset

With luck—must we all give up?
O supernova in this coyote pup—

Operating Manual

Say that you could go out to the grass,
Lie down, and as the light sings past,

Make yourself the sidekick of shining,
Take on transparent life that holds
All others. Say that sky needs a lining

Of dreams. Say that you had learned
How rocketing light depends upon
This wild journeywork, as we return
Our labor to the source, first bond

Of birth and fate, so that as we live,
Nothing stops our loving. Body's mold
Breaks. Who are you, as you give

All there is, in thanks, with adoration?
What is made of light? Soul is detonation.

Corcovado

As water runs from leaf to leaf, so
By clear sweet work, at once you know

Genesis. Thoughts fall to a ground
Of life, red mud of heaven. What is
Holding high this forest, will be found

At the base of your brain. Of this clay
Toucans and monkeys are made, macaws
And iguanas find a form. The worlds say:
Green. Thunderclap. A fresh code of laws

Unfolds—petals, stars, living, dying.
And you say: beauty. For every kiss
Ever given, here is a color. For the lying,

Hatred, misery, comes the jaguar, at last.
This is where our destiny goes to class.

There She Is Again

Across the dawn sky, pomegranate juice
On a white silk sheet, once more the youth

Of light stretches bright limbs, ready
For a labor of beauties and wandering;
Not even frozen hell could hold steady

Before her tease, meditation, dance on dirt,
Mischief, the cut-loose lost-and-found
Fun of her come-hither loving. The ground
Of the world is light, a promise, a flirt,

Learning, touch, story, peace, purpose,
Consummation. History's rancid pandering,
Is nothing to her velocity. Even the dust

Hums a tune for her, works for her trust.
Would we understand, how she loves us?

Falling in Love, and the Invisible World

You who read this, do you ask yourself
About the common, the daily—that shelf,

A necklace, a book, the table, a moment
You notice the wind? Ask yourself, do I
 Love this woman singing in a heaven-sent

Stratospheric hot bar? How incantation
Belongs to her, as she travels in peace,
Cherished; sex and purity in revelation.
Bed-sheets, songs, shot-glasses—a lease

On us they have. They use our lives,
Disappear into permanence. That is why
You must ask yourself, if in your cries

Of love, flesh is soul; whether you
Vanish into life, by what you do.

She Mopped Floors. Was Solitary.

An ordinary woman, who told no one
About her emerald mine, told no one

About how she could see in morning light
A luminous newspaper, and read there
All minute prophecies: this man's plight,

That woman's revelation, bolt of fortunes
In the mind of a baby; the old tambourine
In the pawnshop, whose musicks mean
The coming of a world unseen; the son

Of heaven who works in a tavern pouring
Whiskey to clear the soul; a glossy pair
Of eagles who counsel us, on the restoring

Of a world in love, the world we need.
This woman is world. That world is seed.

It's Merely Physical. Secular.

Will you take a word, and a barrel
Of wine? A phrase, and your feral

Lover, who with spindrift dreaming
Pets and kisses, with a roundabout
Savvy rough cashmere streaming

Touch—your hard cherishing roustabout—
Strokes you into your old-fashioned
Well-known homegrounds, woman. The mount,
Spinning, shock, truth, honey-reasoned

Come-again surprise—detonation, nectary—
You and your lover: what redeeming
Does a day need, save soul's confectory

Of pleasure, a rocketing peace you make—
As you were before you were, you celebrate.

A Waitress I Knew; and You

How the heat of summer stroked her
Open, minute by minute; made her sure

Of what she had learned of final, bold,
Fantastical motions of soul. Her ideas,
Coming on like comets, melt the cold

Repugnant idiocy of men, the glut
Of vomit they call history, their pride
Like cherry candy filled with cyanide.
Doors to the future slammed shut,

Men trying to force the locks—today,
She will come, kiss you, leave the keys
In view, and vanish. My friend, one day

You must choose to live or die. You.
Open the door a world comes through.

When Talk Is World

Your talk a swift river of loving, that
Swings, rushes, dashes, gathers, that

Is ready to return the light entrusted—
Ready to give back in flashing. It's why
A room is radiant around you, adjusted

For the influx of the heavens. It's how
Your momentum in beauty redoes a day
From within, blessed one. It's the way
Your sentences are sparklers, your brow

Calm and even—holding up the sky
Takes constancy in creation. Worlds rely
On your rough jokes, though logic deny

The truth of a woman. What I knew
Of song, of peace, is because of you.

She Is A Genius. This Is Why.

You can live without hope. You can live
Without being loved, days the sieve

Of fortune and care; cold, misbegotten,
Born to the appetite and rapacity of pain.
You can live in these lost days, rotten

With hot glamour of ignorance. Everywhere
Now, that bray—jackass of greed, calling
For company. You know arsenic and stare
Of hatred, men handsome and appalling,

Mutilation in their wallets. You can live
Through all this, my love, soft rain
Will wash your sorrow, you will give

Your hand in trust, will sing and bless:
You have never lost your thankfulness.

One Woman Undoes the Whole Tragic Vision

A house is a mind. This place composes
A world with you. It's why patient roses

Grow from your garden to the sun. Why
Your alpine valley in spring embrace
Of big mountains, spells for the sky

In a pattern of shadow, all the words
A planet is learning to say, every day—
Learning, learning. As your beauty turns
In bemusement through the hours, may

You, my love, find a whirling rhythm,
Make phrases from granite, in grace,
Flourish in the first sun, await within.

We do not work in darkness. You are here
Like a proof of light, planetary and clear.

She Builds a House

When a woman makes a house—when
She sleeps in a canyon and listens; when

The songs of coyotes entrusted to her
Gather at the place of foundation; when
At that place she stands forth to offer

A prayer of thanksgiving, she consults
The radiance of summer, all a spectrum
And jokes and questing, the clear bolts
Of beauty: in savory quicksilver reason

She decides. She knows that to build
She must learn how gusts of heaven
Make and remake this land, milled

Before her on a wheel of stars. In flight,
Yet of earth: a woman's house of light.

The Open Road Loving You

Angels are just those souls who learn
In traveling, mischievous love; who turn

Away from themselves, to see in air
A flourish of invitations. Country roads
Hold a story of coming delicious care.

Little towns call you with a tempest
Of destinations. That sought-for storm
By your candor, will bring you caress—
Red wine on nether lips, firelight warm

On you and your lover. After you stroke
Away the world, laugh at how light goes
Home with us always. Now, you stoke

Your own soul. Step from earth to sky.
In a wind of many loves, learn to fly.

Solemn Policy Declaration

Who sets out to be a clown? No one,
But one day something has to be done:

Peacocks in the kitchen, a black bear
Conducting a symphony, pinwheel galaxy
In the touch of a girl. Who should dare

To live at all? Presume to live at all?
Yet these ocean currents in your hand!
Give them away, give worlds away, fall
Into somersaults, buoyant vaults, to land

On a mountaintop: send your song high
On a gust of laughter. Now it's formal policy:
To joke and muse with god. Dolorous sigh,

Glorious tragic vision, they can have it.
Love rambles off with her molten wit.

Is There An End Of Marveling At You?

What if, love, a pen as light beam
May write the world? As your dream

Is conscious, so the hours of night
Move because of your love, because
Soul has found the origin of sight—

What you see is what you make,
What you mean is the way you give,
Heart we have left to forsake
You wake with beauty as you live—

Peaceable beauty: you say this child
Is all world is, and what earth was.
Perfection is a promise growing wild.

You unfold the fireworks in a word.
We live, because of what you learn.

So. What Do You Mean?

She was so useful, starlight would come
To consult her. Her readers could strum

Her sentences as strings, and hear music
New to this earth, that brought geysers
Out of the ground. Mountain water sick

With expensive garbage, ran sweet. Even
The coyotes came to tease her. When
We arrived with questions, she would send
For angels and vagabonds who would bend

A river of history 'round ideas she has
To give us in rapture. Vicious misers
Wept when her children laughed. The glass

Of this world is on her table, shining, clean.
She would pour the wine of what you mean.

Get Rid of Him

Do you await rescue? By hatred pitched,
Stimulated by your merciless, bewitched

Random, hobnailed world? Poor man,
With your fear like hot tar, your way
A clangor and swagger, your shock-troops

Of complaint like cheap toy soldiers—
Are you rusting in a junkyard of souls,
Scrap metal of heaven, jagged with fears,
Nothing a woman could use? And the foals

In the pasture? Titanic satin of light
On a wilderness river? In a tropical cay
Your warm lover asleep, dreaming, alight—

Will you, at last, undo devouring mind?
World belongs to her. Vanish, and shine.

A Woman You Know

What if she had summer in her hands?
What if in darkness of howling demands,

Swords, inky hatred, a smart committee
For massacre, men's waste, misogyny,
Vainglory, religious loathing—what if she

Still knew a way forward, with solstice
And equinox in the rhythm of her walk?
What if she is delicious? What if a tryst
With her is homecoming, every thought

Is allspice and annunciation? If heaven
Has an address, body and earth progeny
Of paradise most ordinary? Lift and bend

Of a rainbow, the arc of your finding out—
All lead to her, if your life will count.

Where the Desert Leads

My desert, it was because of you
I had a chance to love her, she who

Can walk a wilderness along city streets,
Ideas implacable as ravens, iridescent
Like them—reflecting heaven. The sweets

Of amusement in her mouth—a desert
Prepared me, in tasting her, to recognize
A stardust of story gathered from skies
And from the sand. Beauties men burnt

She kept in a phrase, a rhyme, a song.
She is plain and quiet, phosphorescent.
We see our lies. As world goes wrong,

It will come round to her. The measure
Of life is her mind and musky pleasure.

In the Tropics, She Made a Little Change

What happened to you? I saw no cyclone
Turn in your phrases, nor saw a stone
Turn to an opal in your hand. So, tell:
What transfiguration is this, what befell

Morning, a firestorm of spices? Your eyes,
That mark noon light with your name?
Through the afternoon, through racing skies,
Tropical night and your conjured hurricane,

I follow you. Plain woman, you show
Life candent in close magic: you know
Which comets bring laughter, which crow
Comes from another galaxy. An afterglow

Of brightening soul, lives in your beauty.
Your talk at dusk: honey-glaze on the sea.

When the Newspaper Rots Our Eyes

It was not sorrow, exactly, though the pen
Melted in my hand, while the moldy dead

Gibbered in my face. The wind was full
Of fish guts, a stench of young dead
Mothers, their children filthy and dull

From beatings they receive as slaves.
Not sad today, exactly. Though young men
With weapons once more strut and defend
Us by hanging neighbors for meat. In caves

They leave them to cure, it's the recipe
History knows best, winners well-fed
On tender breasts of losers. Not in misery,

Precisely. Does another century burn?
Would each of us be hatred's intern?

And If Truth Is Not So Felicitous?

A man may awaken, and within himself
Find a rancid, impulsive idiot. We delve

In a land where truth is told helplessly,
As flesh is nothing, body being theater;
In a land not manufactured expressly

By men with big ideas. The smallest gesture
Turns out to count. A woman lifts a glass
Of wine, and a kingdom falls. In a pasture
A shepherd gathers the centuries. In a pass

In the mountains, stories lit up within
By lightning storms are given away. Creator
And firefly, galaxy, syllable, wine-bin—

All this is ours—a world considerate.
I hope to live, when I kill the idiot.

No Original Sin. My Sin.

One day it was repugnant, the clamor
In my head. One day, the running sore

Of my meditations stained so many years,
Phrases, friendships, that at last I left
Myself in the furnace, to raucous jeers.

Now, a hand of peace on my head. I found
That peace has no mercy, what a relief,
For I had earned no mercy. What a relief,
To be forbidden everything, save the ground

Where I had to learn to stand all
Over again, in light, on rock, bereft
Of the glamour of hatred. The daily fall

Is not of Adam. The fall is each of us.
Stop being yourself. Stones are musk.

Am I Doing OK?

I'm fine, except for the icepick of darkness
Driven in my skull. Smart, I don't guess

At the end of the world—it happens each
Day, in the armageddon of daily life.
Such a laugher, that anyone would teach

Us the future holds heaven and hell.
Apocalypse, divinity pack the day,
The worlds at stake in what we say.
Galaxies spin from a miniscule shell

Touched by a woman in love; and I
Remember what I have lost. The fight
Is over. With a little knife they dice

Me for the pan. The eyes make such a mess.
The brain, a toxic, hard pestilent address.

First and Last Terror

I will tell you how a man dies: slowly.
His body makes an example of him. See

The way sunlight shuns him. He talks,
The air forgets him instantly. Words are
Like his body—a beggary. As he walks

Light displays his death in showing
Just how he moves the filth of what
He is. He thinks nothing is owing;
His eyes gnaw, to digest like a gut.

Flesh, words, light: look at him: ask
About terror—a body may be a scar
Left by disease of soul. He may bask

In respect, in security, in family fun.
After such death, flesh shudders on.

A Singular and Daily Apocalypse

Does reality mean anything? What if
The holy beast of success is ours, if

The whole time, working hard, we were
Disciplined, neighborly, life everything
We hoped? We loved shoes, virtue, a stir

Of lavender and tulips in summer wind.
We thought mass murder and discourtesy
Were wrong. So our minute idiocies tend
Evil, ignorance goes demonically free—

A planet charred, mutilation made subtle,
Angels battered and fried; the god-fearing
Rise in joy, to kill a neighbor with shovels—

Educated, happy, this is what we've got.
We never asked what starlight thought.

A Woman Offers Her Son Some Advice

You are your own jailer, in the custody
Of yourself. You trumpet your liberty,

Strut around in a honking game-show,
Roseate days filled with satisfactions
As with sewage. Even a raggedy crow

Flies far, by rhapsody of sweet air,
To prophetic mountains, dwelling-place
Of wakefulness, oldest homeland, where
You will never walk until rough grace

Frees rank heart from your own fist,
Firm there in the fetish and exactions
Of hatred. When is the time, for a tryst

Of truth and flesh, love and the future?
For a jailbreak, you thief, fool, butcher—

Who Needs a Gun To Kill?

A soldier steps on a land mine, and we
See the scarlet fan in the air, he

Is mist and a stump. Back home, men
In offices are moved. O work of policy—
Number, wisdom, word, money, reason—

We have the ultimate weapon: an idea.
A brain is soft, perfect meal for history.
We simmer for days, a stew of victory
Full of pus and speeches. The old mirror

In a house once full of beloved children
Cracks with grief as they die. Liberty!
They say in a smart office. They will send

A patriotic song. You passed the test.
You are the future. History is death.

The Gangsters of Intelligence

Subtle, resolute, correct, lovable, determined,
Riddled by praises; they have shredded him.

Professional, arduous, well-known, powerful:
A shame she was honored, it made her soul
Move like a larva. The two of them masterful,

Phrases danced in the room where they dined,
They dressed in their education, their books
Were mandatory. Their students, slavish, refined,
Got telegrams from the future. The nods, looks,

Given them on this continent, in that city,
Was natural as rain. And like a vein of coal
On fire, their dark essential ignorance, gritty

And infernal, burned superbly out of sight.
Until a shifting of earth in the middle of the night.

The Good Life

All real deaths are suicides. To kill
Yourself, taking every day the pill

Prepared for us—it tastes like custom.
Arithmetic of religion, victory, defeat,
Comfort and misery, each ragged sum

Counted skillfully to our grand total:
Every one a breathing corpse. Dead,
Yet making deposits and being subtle,
Getting what we want, speeding ahead,

Waiting for others to catch up, so we
Sit together, our lives glittering meat
Given each other to cook; let's eat

Our own fresh brains—time to celebrate.
Good is what we do; life, what we hate.

A Cautionary Tale

One thing about the dead: they still love
To dress up, stand straight as a club

In the mirror, carve a smile into place,
Go shuddering into the night. Because
Every night the living dead face to face

Rehearse how they die, how all the gifts
Of heaven, coral, owl, trustworthiness,
Pinwheel galaxy, touch, laughter, hot licks
And the leopard parting the light; breath

And salt and hope—all this was nothing
Beside the one in love with all he does:
Body in a spit-polished mirror. One thing

About the dead: their gangrene of courtesy.
Another thing: they want your company.

A Dynamic Man Muses about Himself

The earth, he understood, was just like
The men and women upon it—like

A piñata. You have to beat it, and
Beat it and beat it before the gifts
Always meant for you fall in sand

At your feet. Still he is thoughtful,
Intense, annoyed; he washes hatred
In hot energies of work—yet, the dull
Papier-mâché of people! Baking bread,

Earning pay, all that whispering, you'd think
They didn't know their own stupid drift
To the day I hang them. You'd think

They'd see I own the gifts inside them—
As they burst open, how I love them.

We Take Their Pill, and Vote

Our adoration, made into votes, takes
A machete to children. Bad luck shakes

A soul from each of them; they give
Themselves, and we dice their hearts.
Government is us, is the way we live,

Lovely in democracy. Mirrors in our rooms
Everywhere are shining, because we all
Think they hold our light. History is cartoons—
Antics of our achievement. We shine, gall

The competition, get smug. What's important
Is that power moves only on our charts.
So we adore our leaders: we whine, rant,

Sing their praises, revel in goodness and wit—
Our cyanide tablets flavored with their spit.

On the Way to His Last Minutes

Your holy book of hatred; a sleepiness
As you strive, daily, in pretence of flesh;
Pride, like sweetmeat in arsenic; anger,
A rat in your heart, eating to reassure

Us with vital signs; sudden tension
And relief, as in puppets; your achievement,
Like sugar rolls with shrapnel. No mention
Of learning, lilacs, the ancient bereavement

When you hit her. All this you must bear.
The angel of death will show you finally
The future in her loving; how sovereignty
Restored overnight her wings; her share

In work of revelation. No one ever cries
For men who abandon their own eyes.

We've Got a Plan

Fill up your hands, pack in your throat
That good gold. Glide on a golden float.
Showtime of gold imperious and shining,
Golden men, the assembly line of smiling—

We are treasure. We are trained, dependable,
Like, say, death. We party in punk houses,
With neon breath, a fancy-dress rabble—
Gas chambers, romance. Ruffled carouses

Ascend, a gold mist, better than clouds.
There, pigs in dangerous streets. Gold
Is Here, our guarantee. We do not mold,
Nor stupidly decompose. Gold crowns

A skull of beauty, skull of perfect power.
Hatred is golden, in this our golden hour.

It's Healthy To Have Close Personal Friends

You give me opinion, words held up
On stilts, like a billboard. You hold up
Your hand, I see a hammer. You stand
In a bar, pounding on friends. In a land

Formed from the paste of you and me,
Where we execrate with fashion, where
We sequin every atrocious idea, history
Swaggers down the runway. We stare,

Go home thrilled, fall down and die,
Fantasize a morning, keep on working,
Calculate finely. We speak when the string
Is pulled, my friend. Puppetry of swine.

But at least we're intimate. This mud
Bubbles with a hell-broth that we love.

Admired Public Speaker

What you construct in yourself, is what
Death is: your choice. You live to gut

Your carcass. It takes decades. You call it
Affection, style, progress. Here and there
Someone notes the peach juice and arsenic—

A ritual drink, so refreshing. You learned
What poison is—it is anything at all
Not connected with heaven. Now you burn.
Nothing temporary can love, only fall

And fall, and say how those flames make
You beautiful. You had a chance: to care,
To call home your first angels, to forsake

The mannequin you are, famous dust—
The showtime of death, here among us.

I Get a Message about my Doom

You do not eat the menu, since you
Know a word is not the thing. Yet you

Eat the world, since you think that
What you see is the world, that
The stage-set of sense is real, that

Rightness, surety, line, mass, forms
Irresistibly given, are waiting for you,
With raw stuffing of energetic charms
To offer themselves on schedule. You

Revel in surface, a fundamentalist. So
Are you doomed. World is not fact.
What you can make and may know

Is to a world bound and seized,
As a solar flare to circus fleas.

Hi! I'm the Angel of Death!

Would you witness sorrow? Be still.
Note heaven just there—a road-kill,

You were going elsewhere. This death
You earned, so resplendent a carcass
Smirking in the mirror. Each breath

Of mint air off the river, gave you
A chance of salvation: death by choice.
Beauty whirled, in love, waiting. But you
Made yourself into meat, made a voice

Of ornament and data. Gifted vulture,
You fed on yourself, in the eating contest
Begun daily. The meal is over. Cock-sure,

You disgust even death. Now let us go,
By your light: sorrow's maggoty glow.

Now For the Bad News

Branding iron: what you have not done
Pressed against your soul. Your homespun

Flesh, all the splendor of the visible
Hung on you, cannot cover the burning—
Hot metal of heedless days. Miserable.

You'll have to kill again. Your tissue
Will halt and harden at death, holding
You still, as you remember what was due
Stars, ocean, this friend, that sparkling—

You remember what you might have loved.
No torment waits for you. There is—nothing,
Just a scar of death indelible, you shoved

In a jar of rancid honey, inside yourself.
Sweet spoiled soul, on some damned shelf.

In Viznar Where They Killed Him

All your life you knew you would be
Murdered. By the side of an olive tree,

Near a sweetwater spring, and stone
Shining with silence, in summer dawn
You stood. You had seldom been alone,

Unless called by color, death, poetry.
Now you stood with a high-school teacher,
And two matadors. Nearby, a door-keeper
Swung open the sky. Of course you need

To talk. And what about a puppet show?
Fascist Catholic thugs said: you belong
To us, especially your ass. Stars rose

In your throat, blood turned to musk—
Lorca, riptide of life, female Jesus.

My Dear Sophisticated Friend

The senses, you say: as if the brain
Is the mind, as though spring rain

Means the same as water. As though
Light is just energy, whether it comes
From the moon, sun on new snow,

Or from a lover's eyes. You say—
What we see is what there is.
Can you count stars at midday?
Do you know what you can give?

Write the equations of a rain forest.
Is a rainbow only angle and sums?
When, in the candlelight, you undress

The one you love, what is it you embrace?
Storybook of beauties, or guts in haste?

It's a Test. Answer Yes or No.

Would you, when comets come through
The room with ideas glittering for you,

Take a ride? These cosmic friends want
Your thriving to hold beauty so perfect
That you may earn a clear, first jaunt

With all wild souls to see new planets—
Such fate summons you, your light
A mantic peace, necessary, full of secrets,
Teasing the darkness. Take the midnight

You have within, yield to dawn light
Rambunctious with destiny, so to connect
You to sacrament, comet, at last a sight

Of your origin, life's permanent address.
Must you seek foolish, heedless death?

A Fundamentalist Has a Bad Day

God takes cash only. More than cash,
She takes what it means. Poisonous trash

In common coin, She knows. A galaxy
In the same coin from another hand,
She knows. The pious stupid minstrelsy

Of everyone who lives to earn credit
With her, She watches with astonishment
And sorrow. We take our first-aid kit
Of virtues, put sterile gauze and unguent

On suppurating hatred of pesky reason.
We slap each other into a righteous band
Sure of credit in our politics and children,

Order, tradition, families rich in trust.
God wants cash. Credit is killing us.

Jokes and the Order of Deep Space

Only if you can, you fraud. It's true,
The morning breeze will bring to you

And to anyone secrets of tigers, ideas
Perfected by labor of lightning-bolts,
Cinnamon theologies, books on how to live

Every minute in this and every world.
A morning breeze will bring you peace—
If you have peace to give. This world,
For you, if you have a world. The sweet

Rambunctious lover, for you, if you
Can love. My dear fraud, all the jokes,
They are on us. What will we do?

A morning breeze: air, light, revelation.
When will we begin our education?

History, If You Will? One Comment—

History, with all due respect, we would
Not offend you, yet what we should

Do, after our studies, is to let you
Know at last—give us your attention,
Try to stay calm—to let you

Know: you are finished. We have learned
The way you mutilate. For you, we
Sipped each other's blood. We turned
Baby girls on a hillside to die. We

Listened, you told us we were nothing.
You said hatred was part of creation.
You said we were meant for suffering.

Well: goodbye. How quickly you die!
You, dark master of the demonic lie.

The Downside. The Upside.

How do you tell if a man is bleeding?
Do you know if the world is feeding?

Did you think nothing was at stake?
Heaven belonged to you, did you think
Love for yourself, life for the sake

Of junk thrills seized, crammed; for
Candied spit of respect, sweet crust
Of time filled with coin, praise, gore—
Did you think it was perfect? Trust:

The world is given on trust. The hours,
Like you, bear sidereal marks. Fates link
Movements of a leopard to city flowers.

Mountains hold the baby; you are
Less than a fly, or more than a star.

The Last Night of Insomnia

Carving knives: those are the thoughts
Insomnia bears. Into coruscating pots

In hell, a neatly cut life goes.
A putrid stew to simmer forever.
In such mind where darkness glows

You know there is no heat like self-
Hatred, as it is nothing but pride.
Self-hatred is the way devils hide;
A taste of guts as you cinch a belt.

Get out of bed, and do anything.
Rid your eyes of death and temper.
Pull the ropes of light, to hear ring

Bells beneath the stars. Then forsake
Yourself; thank heaven you're awake.

You Heavens, I Ask

One candle: I will climb a black mountain
Beyond any map. When I find the fountain

Of youth I will not drink, unless I
Have the chance to give those waters
Away, and ask your leave to die.

I can be my own when I am yours,
When you trust me, then I can
Learn. What is brought to shores
Of earth, I unload in hope, stand

In praise. One candle: as you cast
A seed to grow the future, that cures
Time of motion, I would learn the past

In your forgiveness. To myself dismantle:
My life is yours, if you give me one candle.

Proprietor of Himself

So may you set your willful thought
Aside. A slave revolts. As fools allot

To mischievous, rollicking wind, brute sum,
Scorn, ash, stillness; and proudly arrange
For a holy city, slaughterhouse and slum—

So you had a life. Until a moment when
You knew how any life your own is
Not worth having; how you may ascend
By phosphorescence, in grace; may dismiss

A glossy figure, self-made, painted one,
Imposter who owns you, and now rages
Against whirling liberty. If you have begun

Again, learn to use what you are
As a match you strike to light a star.

Birthmark

Be conscious, but not of yourself. What
Is within you, cosmic birthmark, luck

Of heavens, the mischief of you when
You give, when you make permanent
A skylarking love—what lives, when

Within you, uncanny soul comes forth,
To take a toy of what you were, ghost
Of progress, idea, tiny virtue, course
Of raw sensation—take you at midmost

Of what you hoped, and say: you have
A beginning. As you labor, so repent.
Within flesh is birthmark; a light, path

To star, bed, annunciation, book on a shelf.
Make love conscious, but not of yourself.

They Are Among us, So We Can Live

I have seen them: on the ramparts, a man
In black robes, whose smile could command

Both honey and wormwood, old rubies
And the tissue of hearts. Then a rare book—
When you turn a page, that spring breeze

On your face, you know it is the source
Of spring, of moving white wings, that
Heaven in heart-study, flower as fact.
And I am visited in dreams by a force

Of men and women, who touch the ground
To raise a sidereal house, where they cook
And serve perfection. We hear the sound

Of understanding, lightning and the song
Of what they say, worlds where we belong.

Let's Talk A Little

Life, death, waking and sleep: let's talk
About pattern, resemblance, signs, ought

And is, should, could, rainbows in the arc
Of your lover's hand, in the spring, as he
Caresses you. Upon your body, the mark:

It means heaven. Flesh means: soul.
This world means: a seed. As you live,
My love, where are you led? The coal
That is each day—our senses, give

And take, expectation, drama, reward,
Failure, honor—by what idea and deed
Are diamonds made? Is coal our lord?

Midnight and dawn, spring, the godforsaken—
Light is not asleep. When will we awaken?

The Revel of Forgetfulness

The sun just does her work, unconscious
Of her radiance, of a millennium of trust

Given her by grasses, by mountain ranges
Reveling with her; by a little girl learning
To conjure all the seasons, their changes

Colored and savored—plain cool whisper
Of winter's snowy hypnosis, moist lotion
Of light in summer; spring waters' cure
And cosmos; in autumn pools a potion

Of conscious elixir, whose pattern of silver
Prepares light of dawn. By sun's journey
We have from her all things. We endure

Because she gives and forgets her gifts—
As they are given, as our darkness lifts.

A Morning Told A Man What To Do

This is a way to hope—from indigence.
From poverty, trust, cyclonic resurgence

Of someone who is yourself—someone
You have never known, alive within
Your accomplished cartoon, greedy one

Who, like a monster, wants to keep you
For his own. Flesh and money are clothing.
As you would change your shirt, you
May change your form, by the refolding

Of the spirit-material you are, when
You come to bear another life, to begin
World again, wild with peace; to ascend

Once more. It is today you must make
A star, an earth. For her. For love's sake.

Ordinary Cosmic Door

What if you opened the door
And saw a field of stars? If the floor

Fell away, pinwheel galaxies and comets
Crossed nearby, so you might take
A ride? What if you saw how planets

Spin by clear force of winds that roar
In deep space of your room, winds that
Move because of loving? Close that door.
Look there: your kitchen, a sensuous cat

Asleep on the window sill; everything is
As it was. For heaven's work and sake
Now you know at last how nothing is

As it was. This is where you live:
As no one, with all the worlds to give.

A Homely Guy Makes Good

In your thought, how many crossroads?
In this soil, what star-born law code?

Is there a silence you can taste,
History made for her beautiful hands,
Word constructed of starlight and fate

Come to say where world is hidden,
How soul learns a way home? You hope,
Having lost everything. What is bidden
From your life, just now, as you elope

With her who so many years waited
In the world, who is a world? She stands
Mindful, savory, lustrous; she is mated

To you, you, and you. What will you mean
As you marry this beauty, a world unseen?

You Repent

The meridians of a woman's body are not
World-lines or curve of meteors caught

In flesh. She is a commonplace figure,
Reading a book. Yet today, turning
To you, on her lips you see the sugar:

Grains given her from visiting stars;
Sparkling combed from storm-waves
When in cloud-cover they keep enclaves
Of watchful light: that sweetness barred

To any harvest but the hot movement
Of your hand. In her sugar is learning
Where a world begins. You repent

Everything but your best jokes, your ring,
The way she sweats when she starts to sing.

Walking in Perugia

We saw a stone arch over a street—
In that form we chanced to meet

A bridge that goes from a galaxy to us;
A curve, lovely in sound and sense, in
The way you turn to whisper in trust:

Light never fails anyone; each of us
May fail everyone. At morning an arch
Of stone may move, like an indigo gust
Of remade morning light, that is a part

Of the pleasures of love, both a part
Of the trajectory of heaven, alive within
The morning we walked into our heart.

Stone is earth and idea; one and two.
In this world and another, I love you.

Trying To Be a Good Boy

Never write a poem about reality,
They say—even though pain, scatology,

Conquest and hurt feelings are fine.
Still, that house spinning like a ballerina,
Because of the love within it—the shine

Of trustworthiness on a man—but no, forgive
Me, I will sit here with slapped hands,
I'll write tragedy, okay? Poisonous quicksands
Of history, our daily death-throes, sieve

Of joy which is our ignorance, etc., do I
Pass? Of course, in that bar cold tequila
After a run with wild horses in a hot paradise

Of desert, and your phosphorescent beauties
In bed, spicery of sweat, this morning breeze—

In Her Hands

Jokes, portents, spice, vault of dreams—
One winter afternoon of snow, the seams

Of the sky opened, and a tropical wind
Into the room brought ginger and jasmine—
I am just a man, and I would rescind

Just the man I am. What I have learned
In this wilderness, in the peace of loving
You, is how I have been trying to burn
Wood with sparks on water, trying

To take wing bearing a fine block
Of granite, trying to jewel and defend
The empty box of myself. Every lock

Opens to a key you gave me long ago—
Opens to the season of tropical snow.

Miraculous Biography

One day he saw it, and it disappeared.
More than he hoped, more than feared.

His body was real, yet merest phantom.
Where his life was his own, it was waste.
Then, her dawn light: delicious reason,

Our journey into a peaceable tempest
Of dream, trustworthy wing of language;
Salt, stars, the hope to make a sentence
That moves like a cougar, or an adage

Formed in earth, old rough brightwork
Of understanding. All because of the grace
And incandescence of a wife. He was dirt;

Now, by her trust, his chance, a test,
Song, a daughter. Sun rising in the west.

Six Months Old

With a spiral galaxy inside you, how
Could you be so soft? Our histories bow

To men who dress up death in phrases
And smiles, yet you hold so many joys—
A continent of waterfalls—in the praise

Of your laughter. Little daughter, you live
Centuries every month. You work so hard
Watching this coarse world, trying to give
A grace you bear, in wonder that tarred,

Bleeding history will resist—will resist,
Though as you forgive, what destroys
Us, we can name at last. In the mist

You stand us on rock. Beyond all sorrow,
Your laughter today is peace of tomorrow.

For You

If, together, we had to make a house
On the dark side of the moon, carouse

A way through cold and darkness, light
Old midnight with teasing and red wine,
Until the taste of your musk, my delight,

Meant the homecoming of heat; if
Together, in the tropics, near an iceberg,
On any continent, in any epoch, our ship
Landed us, so you would bring the surge

Of beauty that you are, to that place—
Incendiary soul; lovely in lips and mind,
With wilderness in your touch, grace

And raw goodness in your work: in this life
My song, my trust, is to have you as wife.

Problem of the Signifier, Solved by Baby

The day you said "honey", I knew there
Was hope for language. You made the air

Mean something. The room went silent.
Then we kissed you, your mother and I.
With one word from your paradise sent

You had made morning and the future
Delicious. We saw the way you lived,
At twenty months—how you were sure:
To say is to love. This is what you give.

Our world, word, what you know—
Teach us, my love, how we die
Into your paradise—how we do so

Daily. World, word, what you know:
To be all body, is to be all soul.

Released from Custody

There is no need to tear the churches
Down. All a tormented world lurches

Under weight of ignominy in religion.
Puffed up with poisons, history explodes
In toxic majesty. You stay in the kitchen,

Cooking for loved ones. You are sure.
Churches will be classrooms, concert halls,
An orphanage, a farmers market—no furor
Nor blasphemy, just our life, which calls

For a world waiting these years, watching
Us in hope. It has wild rivers. Mint grows
In family gardens. A friend of yours is patching

A quilt with an ordinary, celestial beauty.
Revelation is ordinary, revelation is duty.

Another Morning with her at Two

It's true, there's a camel in the kitchen
And a bald monk meditating in the den

Next to the storming ocean, but come,
My child, in my arms, we'll see our house
Is ordinary, as we watch dolphins jump

Out the window; when the milkman comes
We'll breakfast with swifts and flamingos,
A haggard angel who needs coffee, the crow
Who can sing at last; over sweet buns,

Fresh juice, raspberries, daughter, loved one,
We'll watch for a whale-spout, and the mouse
Whistling medieval hymns. Lost in reason

On this calm morning, now I'll do the dishes,
As kings and bears come to give you kisses.

Two Years and Six Months, at the Beach

Let them send with notice of my dominion
Over other planets, or the good opinion

Of a council of galaxies. I'm sorry, we
Are building sand castles, the sea breeze
In your hair worth more than all history

Everywhere. Let them offer the velocity
Of mind that makes beauty last—it will
Have to be later, you are running full
Tilt, laughing across gold sand. Let me

Hear paradise delivering happy, cut-
Loose lovely invitations, saying: peace
And wisdom are here, held in trust,

Wild angels are ready for you to meet—
I'll stay, and wash the sand from your feet.

And If Those Clichés about the Ocean Are True?

Scribbling and scribbling of the sea, waving
At you and me, is it true, is there a saving

Grace in sacred trust renewed by hand
Of wind, turning of our earth, embrace
Of moon? Is a book delivered to sand,

Line by line, full of sidereal invention,
Rolling cadence, perfect curves of joy,
Tumult and mist, verses that destroy
Themselves, drawn to iridescent origin,

Once again to come forth in colors
Of young rainbows, there on the face
Of sand, lines simple, earthly, stellar—

Flourish and destiny, as we live and look,
Made over every day, by this holy book.

If You, Who Say You Want Peace

If you, who say you want peace, had
Given you the field of sweetness, had

Air gone miraculous with jasmine, with
Metaphysical promise of fresh bread, word
And grass on summer wind; had the kiss

Inside a dream banish all your fear,
Had the angel rise into your eyes;
If the hand of healing—calloused, dear,
Learned, final—took your hand, to guide

You far, forever from misery of flesh,
Waters of earth ran clear, mind stirred
By wings found beauty at the address

Of starlight, sunlight, soul come true—
Would you then know what to do?

Europe

Finally, love, have you ceased living
On parapets, in poverty, by war-making

And slow public mutilations? Silk robes
Show off malignant centuries. A painting
Of gingered dawn light, loves the roads

Build by slaves who were sons of slaves
And fathers of slaves. Will you stand
Still and listen to stories from graves
Of the slaughtered, give them your hand,

See the loathing in that cause? You
Loved us. Betrayed us. Your educating
Us, we see what it means. We know you.

Do not seek forgiveness. Change yourself.
Start the world again, with everyone else.

It's Just Good Manners

What is our chance, inside of courtesy?
What is blessing? May life be liberty?

May a woman go to assemble a star?
Does all history have the wisdom
Of one seed, the wildflower waiting far

Away in a mid-winter snow pack? Waiting,
But in league with sunlight, because they
Both understand summer.; at work, creating
A nectary and new storm of petals. Day

And night, dirt, bluebird, insect, galaxy
Grass, snowflake, make fantastical sum—
Spiritous planetary calculation. See

What you are given. Send to the address
Of light, a cartwheel of thankfulness.

Don't Just Take a Message. Do Something.

And if light is a signal, always, today
And each second, to birds, children, clay,

Angels, a signal you've been waiting for?
If the world has been calling you home?
If, beyond your labors, you can restore

Yourself to rough irresistible liberty,
You and light? The calling has always
Been present. You hear a hymn of praise
Teaching even the stones about beauty.

The stones are a signal. You, a signal.
This love, a means of traveling, a home,
Our destination. And they talk of a fall?

You know, beyond what they have seen.
Here are words. Live what they mean.

Land of the Life of the Mind

You are meant for work, knowing that
Both sacred canyon and stray cat

Are companions. Idiom of stone, idiom
Of all the animals, all of song is yours,
And in secret. The daily rancid doom,

Social factories to pulverize and can
Men; television of incandescent vomit,
Polite loathing to dice you bit by bit,
Fanatics to swallow you whole—a land

Transfigured in love, miraculous friend,
Offers escape: to form in days the doors
That only a soul can open. We depend

On that labor. It depends on you. Do
Not wait. World in you, must come true—

Madonna and Child, Any Two of Them

Light within them, was light of earth,
And of another world. At her birth

We were students. She taught us how
Flesh is flesh, but recalls paradise. We
Learned how earth is earth, stellar; how

To gather trust, idea, blood, patience,
And love, then in this world to make
A heaven to give away. They meant
To say to us, meant for the sake

Of an original brightness in us: a life
Is goldsmith of its promises. Even grief
Adorns darkness. A raw killing knife

Will cut bread. Child and mother
Show us hope as light shows color.

The Prayer of Her Learning

Goodness is both gravity and grace,
How we hope and fail, what we taste.

The arts of a lover, and in your baby
Brushing through her body every day,
The whole Milky Way. The old and crazy,

By these gifts, will be healed, when they
Learn from you how even ignorance
Once entrusted to beauty, as you pray,
May have its blessed, planetary chance

To suffer into a honey of understanding.
You own what you give. What you say
Has the soft velocity of starlight. Sing

Even to stones, touch heaven's face.
Let gravity everywhere turn to grace.

Just a Book. Just a River

Books are no use, unless you learn
To leaf pages of light, so to turn

Soul loose without rank paraphernalia
Of tiny opinion, bulletin-board of concern,
Neon and clangor, the toy-store regalia

Of yourself. True, a book will not ride
The high country, nor put a blackberry
In your lover's mouth, yet here beside
A bookshelf, this morning, why not marry

Heaven and language? One rhyme, one line
Teach us how history is ready to learn.
Can books move like a river, and shine,

And show, within light, what we may see?
Is earth a soul? And book, a grace at liberty?

Back At Corcovado

Say heaven wanted a workplace, somewhere
Right for quick death and eternity, where

Weather was life and life stand-up tragedy
And comedy in color and music. Say heaven
Wanted a leaf for every chance to go free

Given to you and me, wanted a raindrop
For every beauty offered to hand or eye
Any hour, every hour. She wants it hot,
Exquisite, opalescent. Say heaven was shy,

And wanted to bring together love and death
In naked flourishing, mist and winged reason,
Mask, metamorphosis, poison, elixir; breath

Of trade winds, comment of a typhoon—
Heaven said: rain forest in a full moon.

Corcovado Where You Are

Where, suddenly, a dead leaf on the soil
Becomes soil; where the brutish coil

Of a snake whose venom melts diamonds
Is so beautiful, it teaches the future
About pattern and power, about reasons

Paradise is diabolical; where rain is friendship
Gone free: a banter, tumultuous and candid
In the barroom of the heavens, all a gift,
Boisterous philharmonic confabulations, bid

And cry, experiment, provocation, sonnets,
The declaration of a lifetime: this is rain, pure—
Only sentences that count. A forest that forgets

Everything but life. Forever, as you talk,
Make a tropics within, wherever you walk.

After a Week's Absence, a Little Girl

Imagination fails, because her softness
Is beyond memory, sleep beyond rest,

Even rest of heaven on the seventh day;
Because vision, even if it rocks you
Awake before dawn, is mute and gray

At her wink, her phosphor gone free;
Because imagination fails, before her flesh
Of far-rambling, fierce-winged soul. She
Is four years old. In a yellow dress

She walks across the grass; the old light
Stops to watch. What all of us once knew,
She safeguards for our joy, as her sight

Searches in soil, rustles up a galaxy—
The flesh of revelation, imp of liberty.

How This One Man Died

There were seeds in his bone-marrow.
Flowers split bones. We split with sorrow.

A tornado of light took him away.
Slanting rain with his phrases shone,
His strong hands are kittens at play.

We pray in darkness, as his thoughts
Go wandering—childhood cotton candy,
Baseball games and war games, rocks
Of a thousand mountains. In wild integrity

He can be anything. His planted days
Detonate in those seeds, to be grown
Each one to another world. Still, he plays—

As lovers wade into a tropical river:
On skin, sweet wind—secret grace-giver.

Every Night

By candlelight, every night, I watched you.
Your sentences connected stars. Into view

Came a constellation of our loving, season
By season, hour by bright hour, my beauty,
Hot rhapsodist and trickster of reason,

Acrobat of metaphor, clown tossing jokes
Into the air, for the cats to catch
In animal happiness, as grace revoked
All rank grim pieties. In our match

Was rain forest, raucous peace. Stories
Cartwheeled across the table; our liberty
Went on the wings of trust, on a breeze

We knew was blessing. Candlelit life-giver,
Telling stories in a cabin by a green river.

For My Oldest Friend

It may be that you had some beliefs,
So many kittens raised and released

To see if they would play with history.
But at the end of belief, I saw in you
A new world, made with sovereignty

And jokes, because you put yourself
To work, in terror, then in understanding:
Hatred cooks with ignorance, demanding
Filet of human hearts, since the shelf

Has centuries of recipes. You always thought
We should dine elsewhere; that through
Paradise present, secrets we have sought

Will come into our hands, as we labor.
In every decent man, you saw a savior.

Time For the End of Time

There is no time—no time. A life,
Lovemaking, signal mysteries; world rife
In cougars, hopes; girls supple in miracle;
Prisoners eating fresh brains. Yet a lyrical

Long motion in roughhousing sea wind
Never undoes its ebullience, the ravens
With syntax of desert sand, cry to send
A coolness of mind into our seasons

Of heat—no time, there is no time.
Does the sea rest? Love, give the wine
Of what you do away forever. Go to refine
Sand of history into gold. Then shine:

Body is soul, man woman, all of time
Is circulation of world in heart's design.

What If It's True?

What if it's true, that morning light
Is directory of paradise? That birthright

Is to tease heaven, by finding earth?
You have learned from a red-tailed hawk
All a university of vigilance. You search

For a stone-cut sentence, or verse ready
To hold the wings you need for work.
Learn, in hammering hours, to hold steady,
Because it's true: rainbows in the dirt

Mark our trail; a river has taught you
By its turning, how to braid each lock
Of your lover's shining hair. It's true:

Because of loving her, now the dawn
Seeks in you permanence and her song.

Worlds and Words, You and Earth

Where, if you found the angel inside you,
Would she unfurl her wings? Continue,

For only world has space enough, only
Our life made of earth is big enough,
Only the star-burst of blessed secrecy

In a word will shine enough, to hold
A motion of light that makes the wings
That carry your incarnation. The gold
That comes again to your eyes, brings

To your vision what is permanent here,
Within you, everywhere. Satin and rough,
Minute, infinite, brief, pathetic, dear,

You are born here. Your body a pen.
Write your story: escapade of heaven.

That Old Chestnut Again

Reader, I come with a common message.
It cannot belong to me; I am a carriage.

Within a word moves light, who would
Travel with you. I hope you might
Sing with me. What on earth is good

Seeks you, as a cyclone seeks wind,
Grace seeks a dancer, an old story
Seeks understanding. Beloved, my kin,
You are come because of the glory;

Invited here, all worlds left open.
Listen: When you can move the light
Along the mountain, on that day, then

You will move the mountain. Come true—
Conceive the light; light conceived you.

Who Is It Who Lights the World?

And who, as talk goes over the tables
At evening, cannot love clear fables

Called forth by candlelight. That flame
Knows us. We are just such burning,
A body of fire, drawing on world, game

And giving, and so by company, room,
Love and phrase; by a beloved minutiae
Of history, this beginning. Yet what doom
If you give light only, not the luminalia

When your flame touches another wick
In readiness. In that story of learning—
Incendiary peace. From life as candlestick,

You gather life, then from light detach—
Fire that learned how to be a match.

OK, Now I Have A Question

Not the tapestry, but an intelligence within
The thread. Not the painting, but the occasion,

The afternoon of creation, the way a painter
Loved you, and loved what you love.
Not the wilderness, where you, at the center

Of the world, cartwheeled in exultation,
But our silken tumult of paradise, raucous
And classical—music, irresistible revelation,
All an origin and future. The hour conducts

Mountains, moths, wind, bristlecone pine
And wildflowers, waterfall, black bear cub,
And work comes when you ask: if wine

Is made of grapes, light made of the sun,
What is made of you, by heart's gestation?

Because

Because love is a place. Green river,
The shadow of your hand, the stature

Of dragonflies in late honeyed light
In a canyon of sacramental mood; a fox,
Her coat collecting softness; a midnight

Where you and I walked, as mockingbirds
Marked air in amusement; your gardens
Giving back beauties—you stood, learned,
Plants leaned into your touch. You opened

In work, a world of air and wing.
Blackberries ripened in our jokes. Talk
Is a place. Joy is a place. Bring

Hope; entrust memory to grace.
Life comes home. Love is a place.

Even If

Even if you are despised and weary,
Before the mirror now sick and leery,

Even if you are filled with contentment,
Personal candy of peach, mint, sludge;
Even if medals on your shirt have bent

Your body, broken your memory, even if
You have polished and polished sorrow
In hopes of making it shine like a cliff
Of beautiful obsidian, so that tomorrow

You have a place to climb, and jump;
Even if you have been a killing drudge,
In your hand a knife, your mind a sump—

Even as you suffer, as the worlds end
Lift sail for the bright wind of heaven.

Finally, Women Take Power

You would not fly on the one wing
Of reason, nor suffer the story of a king

Without an irrepressible queen, rough
In wit and rough in bed. You would
Not suffer hand or mind to handcuff

Man to woman, one word to another,
One world to another—you've made
A vow to undo destiny. You've bade
The little boys who order us to suffer

To put down their guns and go back,
Be quiet, start over, conjure the good—
Or at least to stop working on the rack

Where they stretch history and earth.
Because of you, life will come first.

The Weather of A Young Woman

Weather is within. You see lightning,
Soft rain, cyclones; flaunt and sing

Of hard snow at half-moon, a wind
From world's end. All this is tissue
Of yourself. You love, sing; you begin

To travel earth as weather. It is so
Because there is no separation; because
This atmosphere is ideas. Thunder grows
From a sonnet you loved. Hack-saws

Of an ice-storm, working hour by hour,
As you sleep, rip your life in two.
On a window, frost dreams a flower.

You are moonlight. You are more.
You have a calling. The world is a door.

Just Now Is

The last moment of your last afternoon
On earth, with tanager, tidal wave, moon,

Crows who perch on shoulders of saints,
The handful of ashes that a child mixed
With water, mud and mystical paints,

To make a ripe persimmon; with rain forests
On a coast, hiding place for young galaxies
In transit—someplace they can rest
A billion stars as insect eggs; with liberties

Of wind in league with water and light
Making on coastlines, lakes, rivers, quick
In the rough way of the sacred, for our sight,

Jewels of the next world: it's the moment—
Put out your thumb for the comet.

Coming Here

A castaway—though I remember a city
Full of pinwheel galaxies, laughs, honesty,

The original tiger; it has trust and colors
For which, here, we have no names, ideas
Of power, phosphor, hope, motion so pure

It does nothing but make beauty visible.
It is motion that does not mark time,
But life that is permanent within design.
Past is future. A peach, the moon. Sensible

Is real. Pandemonium, music. Questions
Go to bed with understanding. The seven seas
Have a meal together. But then the directions,

A journey to earth, lovely costume of clay—
This bright suffering, joy of the castaway.

You Mean We Have to Choose?

What will it be, springtime or five-star generals?
Golden eagles or terrified soldiers, gun-barrels
Lovesick for a child to fire at. How will you live?
Can lightning bolts tell a joke? What will you give

In trade for the emerald in a girl's good sense?
When a vagabond from heaven stops in, will you
Speak to her in the dialect of twilight, and sense
In her, how where she walks the day is new:

Her steps are skylarking, earth, air; she is home—
What will you do? Can you serve today as sidekick
To your lover on a trapeze between planets? Wick
Of a candle held up inside the heart that shone

With weathers of devotion, as you watch rise
The candle of the sun in the heart of the skies?

A NOTE ABOUT THE AUTHOR

Steven Nightingale is the author of two novels, *The Lost Coast* and *The Thirteenth Daughter of the Moon*, and *Cartwheels*, a limited edition book of sonnets, and *The Planetary Tambourine: 99 Sonnets,* published by the Black Rock Press. A native Nevadan, he received a B.A. at Stanford University where he studied computer science and literature. After living in Spain for three years, he has now resettled in the Santa Cruz mountains near Woodside, California, with his wife Lucy and daughter Gabriella.

COLOPHON

Designed and produced by Bob Blesse at the Black Rock Press,
University of Nevada, Reno. The typeface is Dante, designed
by Giovanni Mardersteig. The display font is Rialto designed by
Giovanni de Faccio and Lui Karner in Austria. Printed and bound
by Thomson-Shore, Inc., Dexter, Michigan.